A Whole & Nourished Life

6 weeks of soul nourishing truth

Danielle Porter

Name: Danielle Porter
Title: A Whole & Nourished Life, 6 weeks of soul nourishing truth
By Danielle Porter
Identifiers: ISBN: 978-1-952369-45-2
Subjects: 1. Religion/General
2. Religion/Christian Living/Devotional
3. Religion/Christianity/Personal Growth

Cover Designer: Krystine Kercher
Back Cover Color Food Photos: Erica Trout
Photo Credits: Page 118

Published by EA Books Publishing, a division of

Living Parables of Central Florida, Inc. a 501c3

EABooksPublishing.com

Couple of Quick Things

Before I even begin, I have to express my deepest gratitude for the people that encouraged me to press onward in writing this devotional. First, thanks be to God, without Him there would be none of this. Second, to my husband, a true gift from God; Matthew you are always my biggest supporter. You're the one who pushes me to use the gifts God gave me and never tells me I've lost my mind when I come up with a new idea. To my friends and mentors, CC Davis, Jennifer Hynes, Brooke Richie, Jaclyn Hughes, and Maggie Marlow. You women are the best #hypesquad a girl could ask for. I would have quit 100 times without your encouragement and support. And finally, to EA Publishing, your team is what pushed this from just words on my computer to something fit to share with the world. I am forever grateful.

Finally, each week in this book has three unique features. I didn't include them on accident, so lean in, give them a shot. At the end of every five days there is a journaling page. Feel free to use it throughout the week too, so you can see how your understanding of each concept changes as you dive deeper. Each week I give you a prompt to think about incorporating into your life. I'm not telling you to, but merely suggesting options to find Sabbath rest in your crazy busy life. The second unique inclusion is a recipe to nourish your body. Food brings people together. So, if you're completing this devotional with a group, consider making the recipes for your meeting!

In 2014 I gave birth to a beautiful baby girl. Even though I already had a son who I loved more than I even realized was possible, there was something about having a girl and being a female that shattered me. I had these panic moments that she was going to turn out just like me. She would endure the same self-loathing, the same poor self-image, the same defeats, and I couldn't handle it. I confided in a trusted friend and she gave me a simple answer. "Then change who you are into someone who, if she turned out like you, you'd be proud of."

And it truly was that simple. It wasn't easy, not by a long shot, but it was simple. It was about intentional living and little by little I made those changes in my physical self (the way I ate and the exercises I started doing), but what I found, and what I hope to convey here, is that so much of a physical journey is mirrored in our spiritual journey. As my body changed, so did my soul.

I'm a woman, I'm a mother, I'm a Christian, I'm a friend, I'm a health coach, I'm a sinner, I'm imperfect. I'm most likely just like you. What I don't need (and you don't either) is another book telling us what we're not doing enough of and instructions on how to "optimize" our life. The last thing any of us need is another instruction manual. So that's not what you'll find here.

I grew up in a Southern Baptist church in Virginia filled with women's groups, Bible studies, potlucks and "bless her hearts." The salads were mayo-filled and most of the time there were more pies at the potluck than there were main dishes. While all of that is well and good, perhaps we can do a little better. Perhaps we can focus on spiritual growth and physical health. Perhaps we can nourish our whole life instead of segmenting it.

I'm glad you've picked up this book because while I'm not here to offer you an instruction manual, I am here to offer you hope, grace, and a cozy spot to sit and think.

I'm here to enter a space that is often times either filled with either "never good enough" criticism or "you are enough" platitudes which prevent spiritual growth. I'm here to enter into a space that can be so focused on spiritual growth it neglects to acknowledge God does care for your body and how you attend to it.

I wrote this book with women's groups in mind. I included six of my favorite healthy recipes so you and your growth partners can bring something healthy to the next meet-up. I promise, there's room for nourishing food right alongside the pies!

I pray this book calls you forward. I pray it challenges some long held beliefs. I pray it causes you to think and question. Fair warning, for me, the giant red flag for growth comes with a healthy dose of defensiveness. So don't be surprised if you want to close the book and say things like "she doesn't even know me," eyeroll, eyeroll, eyeroll. come on, you don't know how ___ I am.

Stick with me friend. Growth is worth it. You are worth it. Not because I said so, but because God says so.

Contents

Part 1
Becoming a First Fruits Woman

Week 1
Becoming a First Fruits Woman

Day 1
What does it mean to give your first fruits?

Proverbs 3:9-10 (ESV)

Honor the Lord with your wealth and with the first fruits of all your produce; then your barns will be filled with plenty, and your vats will be bursting with wine.

In 2017, I became obsessed with the concept of first fruits. It happened in our small group Bible study leader's house. I shared how I had been challenged in my health coaching business to begin waking up early and devoting time to a "morning process." One of the other women in the group asked, "Where is God in all of that process?" It began as a simple question, but led me to deepen my understanding of who I really wanted to begin my day with.

In an agriculture-based culture like that of the Old Testament, first fruits meant something quite different than it typically means today. In harvest time, a time to reap what you sowed, you gave your first fruits to the priest (Leviticus 23:10) as a sign of faith; a sign that you trusted God would provide, not only economically but for you and your family's daily sustenance. Moses first brings up the idea of first fruits in Exodus and then goes on to mention it twelve more times. So this is obviously something God wants us to take note of. Just like when you repeat yourself over and over to your children, you want them to take notice. God's that way too.

The concept of first fruits is easy to dismiss as an "Old Testament colloquialism" that doesn't apply to 21st century people such as you and me. Most of us don't have a harvest growing in our back yard that we could sacrifice the first fruits from. However, we do have something precious to offer, something everyone, from your kids to your spouse to the random strangers on the Internet, are clamoring for: your time and attention.

We'll continue talking more about first fruits this week, but for now sit with the idea that no matter what you believed prior to starting this book, you most definitely do have first fruits and those around you want them.

1

Discussion questions:

How do you feel the concept of first fruits applies to your life today?

What do you see as your harvest?

Day 2
What are your first fruits?

2 Chronicles 31:5 (ESV)

As soon as the command was spread abroad, the people of Israel gave in abundance the first fruits of grain, wine, oil, honey, and of all the produce of the field. And they brought in abundantly the tithe of everything.

While we might not have grain, wine, oil, or honey in our back yard to sacrifice, we do have something incredibly precious: our time and attention. From the moment our eyes flicker open in the morning, our time and attention are in demand. First from our alarm clock, usually our phone. The red notification dots demand we click and see what happened while we were sleeping. Eighteen emails unread, four direct messages waiting to be seen. If we're in a life space where we're constantly awakened by a baby or toddler, it's obvious where those screaming demands are coming from. Our time is so often not our own, unless... unless we make a conscious, intentional effort to set aside that time as a sacrificial offering to God.

Personal development gurus will tell you the first hour of your day is the most important. That "successful" people don't give other people the first hours of their day. Successful people use them to pour into themselves so they show up as the best version of themselves for others. They do this so they can sell the most real estate or face cream or even simply become the most patient mother. I have to say I totally agree. But instead of pouring into ourselves from a cup that will always run dry (the world's cup), we have the choice to pour into ourselves from God's cup. The cup that never runs dry.

Sacrificing our time and our attention before they are sullied by the demands of others, gives God first dibs on us. Doesn't He deserve that? After sacrificing His son as first fruit (1 Corinthians 15:20), doesn't He deserve the first fruit of our day?

3

Discussion Question:

Currently what part of your day is sacrificed to giving your time & attention to God?

How does your concept of becoming a first fruits woman change when you consider what your first fruits might be?

Day 3
Sacrifice

2 Samuel 24:24

But the king replied to Araunah, 'No, I insist on paying you for it. I will not sacrifice to the Lord my God burnt offerings that cost me nothing

What does sacrifice really mean? Sacrifice is giving up something important in order to gain something of more importance. When I first heard about sacrifice in this way, I was not in a life space where this rubbed me the right way. I was sitting in the living room of our small group Bible study leader's house and my defenses immediately went up. The question was asked, "are you really sacrificing something for God?" I rolled my eyes, because most of the time that question can lead to a #humblebrag competition. Who has sacrificed the most? "I really needed that $20 but instead I gave it in the offering bucket." "Oh yeah, I stopped on the side of the road and helped a stranded car and it made me late for dinner." And on and on until someone busts out something "sooo sacrificial" we all can't "one up" them.

Thankfully, our group leader immediately discussed the important role of obedience in sacrifice. Are you listening to what God is asking you to sacrifice?

God started an itch I couldn't stop scratching. "God, I felt like I was sacrificing something to you. I could be doing loads of other things during my kids' nap time, but instead I sat down to read my devotional and the Bible for a few minutes" … that is, if I didn't get distracted by my phone dinging or the mountains of laundry on the couch beside me.

Let's go back to the definition of sacrifice: giving up something important in order to gain something of more importance. Giving up something important causes a point of pain. Romans 12:1 tells us, "Therefore, I urge you, brothers and sisters, in view of God's mercy, to offer your bodies as a living sacrifice, holy and pleasing to God—this is your true and proper worship."

When we feel the pain of our sacrifice then we know we are really giving up something important. Is what I gave up an actual sacrifice or just something I did to check off on my daily to-do list? Is what I gave up causing me to put my faith in God's provision?

Discussion Questions:

This is a personal question, not a one-upping contest question, Is what you're sacrificing causing you any type of pain?

If not, what is God calling you to sacrifice?

Day 4
Sacrifice is an everyday occurrence

Matthew 16:24 (ESV)

Then Jesus told his disciples, "If anyone would come after me, let him deny himself and take up his cross and follow me."

In the "personal development" circles I run in, consistency is preached over and over and over. Really until it's run into the ground. But consistency is preached for good reason. Doing something inconsistently doesn't yield consistent results. No matter if it's eating healthy foods, exercising or spending time with the Lord, irregular behaviors don't breed regular results. Your consistent relationship with chips and fast food is not going to give way to a pants' size you're comfortable in. In the same way your inconsistent Bible opening isn't going to breed a deep understanding of God's word.

We are all seeking the magic pill. The pill that sends us into fat burning mode where we don't have to practice actual healthy behaviors to lose the weight. A pill providing intimacy with God and a Christ-like-mindset without actually having to crack open the Bible or sacrifice any of our fleshly desires. I've worked in the health industry for over six years now, and I'd be lying if I said I wasn't tempted at times to get behind the newest fad of "fat burning coffee" or "detox" tea. It'd be so much easier to sell my clients a magic pill which will produce quick little results, than it is to teach them sustainable lifestyle practices. But I can't wholeheartedly get behind anything that doesn't align with God's design, and the last time I checked, quick fixes aren't biblical.

Magic pills just aren't reality. They are a façade Satan uses to lure us into believing we can keep "ourselves" and still gain Christ. But the Bible repeatedly tells us this is false. First John 2:16 (ESV) reminds us, "For all that is in the world—the desires of the flesh and the desires of the eyes and pride in possessions—is not from the Father but is from the world." Daily submission is the only way to true intimacy here. And just like the box of chocolate cookies so easily inhaled, grace abounds. God knows we'll be inconsistent, but we can set our hearts in a submissive posture and let God reign.

Discussion Questions:

In what area of your life do you most struggle with consistency?

How have you tried to force consistency?

Day 5
Praying for consistency

Psalm 119:33 (VOICE)

O Eternal One, show me how to live according to Your statutes, and I will keep them always.

Psalm 119:33 gives me hope. If David, the King of Israel, a man after God's own heart, David, commander and chief of God's army.... If he has to pray for God to help him be consistent, then there is no shame in my prayer. There is no shame in crying out to God for Him to help me be consistent in pursuing a nourished life.

A good New Year's resolution to submit to God isn't enough. We will not constantly live on mountaintop experiences such as the women's conference high or the Sunday morning post-worship euphoria. Instead, we can pray and ask God to develop in us a disciplined daily pursuit of His way.

I will never forget the night I started praying for God to wake me up when my alarm went off so I could spend more time with Him. Do you know what our good Father did? He woke me up fifteen minutes before my alarm went off to the sound of the cat hacking up a hairball on my side of the bed. Well let me tell you, that was the last time I prayed that prayer! LOL. Just kidding... kind of.

Sacrificing to God the first fruits of our time and energy takes discipline. That's not something we can just will into fruition most times. We need divine intervention...or at least I do. I'm not strong enough on my own. I'm not "enough." If I were, I wouldn't need God. And isn't that ultimately the point of it all? To remind us we actually aren't the point? Only God is the point!

Discussion Question:

Do you think you can be consistent on your own without divine intervention?

Have you ever felt silly praying for help with consistency? Why?

JOURNALING PAGE:

How did your concept of becoming a first fruits woman change throughout the week?

_____

_____

_____

_____

_____

_____

_____

_____

_____

_____

_____

_____

_____

_____

_____

_____

_____

_____

_____

_____

_____

_____

Grace Day

Use this day to catch up on any days you might
have missed this past week or just spend time
lingering with God In your morning process

Figure 1.1

Day 7
Restful Reminder

Social Media Sabbath is something my husband and I discovered in 2017 that really helped us understand what a Sabbath could mean for us in modern day. It didn't seem feasible to us to completely shut down everything and not participate in life, or sit in a quiet, dark house for twenty-four hours with two small children. Running a business that relies on social media makes it easy for me to get sucked into continually occupying space there. Being available for my clients and coaches is an important part of my business structure. But it seemed to be leaching into all the cracks and crevices of my life. Yet the idea of turning it off permanently didn't appeal to me.

So we decided to take a small step toward practicing a Sabbath rest by choosing to turn off social media for 24 hours. From 3pm Saturday afternoon until 3pm Sunday there is no social media, no TV, no electronic devices at all. We disabled the apps on our phone (google how to do this for your brand of phone, it's a life-changer). We lean into our life in the present: we snuggle together, play games, take walks, and pray together without the background notifications dinging.

Will you give some real thought to building in a social media Sabbath each week? You might find it truly refreshes your soul.

Figure 1.2

Figure 1.3

Recipe: Carrot Cake Oatmeal Muffins

These Carrot Cake Oatmeal Muffins are a healthy and nutritious way to start your day!

Prep Time 15 mins
Cook Time 30 mins
Total Time 45 mins
Servings 12 servings, approx. 1 muffin cup each
Calories 105 cal

Ingredients

- 2 cups dry old-fashioned rolled oats
- 1 tsp. baking powder
- ½ tsp. ground cinnamon
- ¼ tsp. ground ginger
- ¼ tsp. ground nutmeg
- ¼ tsp. sea salt (or Himalayan salt)
- 1 cup unsweetened coconut milk
- 2 large eggs, lightly beaten
- ¼ cup pure maple syrup
- 1 tsp. pure vanilla extract
- ¾ cup grated carrots (approx. 1¼ medium)
- ¼ cup crushed pineapple, in 100% pineapple juice, drained
- 3 Tbsp. light sour cream
- 3 Tbsp. powdered sugar

Instructions

1. Preheat oven to 350° F.
2. Prepare 12 muffin cups by lining with muffin papers. Set aside.
3. Combine oats, baking powder, cinnamon, ginger, nutmeg, and salt in a medium bowl; mix well. Set aside.

4. Combine coconut milk, eggs, maple syrup, extract, carrots, and pineapple in a medium bowl; mix well.
5. Fold coconut milk mixture into oat mixture; mix well.
6. Divide batter evenly into prepared muffin cups.
7. Bake for 30 minutes, rotating pan after 15 minutes.
8. While oatmeal cups are baking, make icing. Combine sour cream and powdered sugar in a small bowl; mix well. Set aside.
9. Let oatmeal cups cool in pan until you can handle them. Remove to a cooling rack.
10. Drizzle each oatmeal cup with approximately 1 tsp. icing before serving; serve warm.

Recipe Notes

As soon as oatmeal cups are cool, place in an airtight container and store in the refrigerator for 1 day. If storing longer, place in the freezer for up to 3 months.

For full color photos and step by step visual instructions please visit www.daniellemporter.com/recipes

Week 2
Discipline

Day 1
Posture of submission

James 4:7

Submit yourselves, then, to God. Resist the devil, and he will flee from you.

Oh, submission, such a funny little word. If you say that word to the wrong women, you might end up with a black eye. I mean we all know that woman, right, the one who as soon as we start talking about submission, crosses her arms, purses her lips, and you can read her thoughts clear as day on her face. "I ain't submittin' to no one, no way, no how, and especially no man." Oh sweet friend, I've been there. Submission for submission's sake isn't ever worth it. But submission out of love? That's a different story.

Isn't submission what the Bible calls for? Isn't it the prescription for all things? James here tells us submission to God revokes the devil's microphone privileges in our life. I find when I try to subvert the hierarchy of control in my life and grab the reigns again, it never ends well. I fight and struggle and run myself dry trying to sit on the throne. The reality is that only God deserves that throne. When we flip this upside down and put ourselves up there, submission is downright impossible. Why we can't just get the idea the first time is a mystery to me. I experience this on a daily basis and have to submit myself over and over to the ultimate authority of Christ.

Funny enough, the posture of submission is something I learned in my yoga practice. Put the book down at the end of this paragraph and do me a favor, get down on the floor in child's pose. If you're not familiar with child's pose, you'll want to start on your hands and knees, sink your hips down towards your feet, arms out in front of you, face down (or turn your face to the side if that's more comfortable). You're in full on child's pose. Now pray, talk to God for a few minutes in this position. It's a completely different experience for me than sitting in my comfy chair with a cup of coffee. My submission level is at an all-time high in that position. It seems silly, but submitting this way has truly changed my relationship with God. I find myself more humble, less likely to try to take the throne on a daily basis. Try it!

Discussion questions:

Did you do child's pose prayer?

Did this change your posture toward submission?

How did physically changing your posture effect your heart posture?

Day 2
Consequences

Romans 2:5 (ESV)

But because of your hard and impenitent heart you are storing up wrath for yourself on the day of wrath when God's righteous judgment will be revealed.

Well now, this is going to be a fun week isn't it? First, we talk about submission, and next up is the wrath of God… funsies! It's not sexy or fun, but it's truth. And I'm not interested in anything less than the full Gospel truth in the word of God. Culture tells us we're perfect, we were made this way, baby you were born this way, you're enough.

Oh friend… no. We're not perfect, we're not enough, and you wanna really be mad at me… you were born a sinner. Sorry to shatter the world's "make you feel good" voice. I know, I'm no fun, am I?

There are eternal consequences for our hard hearts. Just as Paul says in Romans 2, there are actual consequences for our stubbornness. And it's not pretty. I could gloss over this and make it a little prettier, but the reality is the consequence of the wrath of God. And just like eating a cheeseburger for lunch a few times a week, the consequences are not immediate. So much of my physical health journey has mirrored the revelations in my spiritual life. It's not the massive steps that move us away from Christ usually, just like it's not the individual binge eating episodes… it's the cumulative effect of daily decisions. It's the slow hardening. The daily decision (and yes, friend, it is a decision) to listen to what the world says about us that brings God's wrath. It's the small overages and the workouts we skip that add up big in our health and it's the small voices you listen to that add up big in our spiritual life.

Our decisions do absolutely have real life tangible consequences. And while in the present moment we don't see those consequences as important; I can't emphasize enough the gravity of our decisions. To take it back to yesterday's chat, the daily decision to get back up on our throne for the 2,918,301 day in a row pulls us further from the beautiful glorious relationship with God.

And to clear up my position on the "you are enough" movement... no, my heart is set on truth and I can't allow myself to take any less of a stance. If we were enough, if we were perfect just the way we are, there would be no need for God. We'd be our own God. There would be no purpose in life. And that's just not reality. You were "born this way"–friend we were born sinners. It's only through the redeeming love of Jesus Christ that we are saved, not by anything we've done, but through what He did on the cross.

Discussion Question:

What small decisions are you making daily that you are turning a blind eye to the consequences of?

This is not about condemnation; that's the devil's work. It's about conviction, that's the work of the Holy Spirit.

Day 3
Discipline sucks

Hebrews 12:11

No discipline seems pleasant at the time, but painful. Later on, however, it produces a harvest of righteousness and peace for those who have been trained by it.

I truly believe nothing revealed God's love for me more than when I became a mother. Other characteristics of God were shining bright, but not God the Father. When I became a parent, it was an awakening of sorts to this characteristic of God. All of a sudden I understood discipline and pain and obedience and love in a whole new way. When you have to discipline your child, you're standing there explaining to them why the discipline is necessary. But let me tell you, those sweet angel children of mine… they.do.not.care. They just don't. Arms crossed, feet stamping, threatening to burst into a full-blown tantrum kinda do not care. And as their mother I'm like, FOR THE LOVE WILL YOU PLEASE JUST DO _____ then we can go have fun, we can do all the great things, I can give you all the great things. I JUST NEED YOU TO OBEY. But those strong-willed suckers won't budge. Then I have to issue punishment, which if you're a parent you know is necessary, but it just stinks. Because no one likes to be the mean parent. But discipline is required when obedience isn't immediate. And all of a sudden my eyes were opened. OHHHH I get it God. I get the discipline. I get why discipline is painful. If I had just obeyed from the beginning, I wouldn't be in this predicament now, would I? Oh, how the lessons echo through my heart now.

The other way this was echoed was in my physical journey. In 2014 my husband and I decided to change our lifestyle. You can read more about my health journey in later weeks of this study, but other than parenthood, my journey to better health has deepened my relationship with Christ more than anything else. The parallels between getting up early to exercise and the discipline it takes to follow God … unmatched. The parallels between NOT giving into every food craving and not giving into every sinful temptation … unmatched. The parallels between gateway foods and gateway "tickle sins" as Drew Dyck calls them in his book, Your Future Self Will Thank You … unmatched.

Discipline does suck. It is painful. Sometimes gut-wrenchingly painful. But it's so necessary. And the best thing I know to do is submit myself to the sovereignty of God as my Father, who has never ever failed me. He always sees the bigger picture.

Discussion Question:

Is there a memory you can reflect back on and see now how even though the discipline was painful, God's hand was sovereign?

Is there anything, any step of obedience, you can see now that should have been taken earlier?

Day 4
Self-discipline

2 Timothy 1:7

For the Spirit God gave us does not make us timid, but gives us power, love and self-discipline.

This verse is so powerful, right? We are powerful. We are loving. We are self-disciplined. I am woman, hear me roar! I'm breaking out into some kind of powerful ballad right now about how insanely powerful I am. But wait. We skipped a part, didn't we? For the Spirit of God, well shoot. So I've got to have the Spirit of God in me in order to tap into that power and love and self-discipline. It's not ME. Shoot there it is again, the big voice of God with his big megaphone telling me, "You're not the point." Well dang.

Self-discipline is something I tried (and miserably failed) at for so many years of my life. I'd get a bug and start a new habit, reading my Bible, exercising, laying off the Twinkies … and inevitably I'd fail. Until one day. I learned. The best way to have self-control is to turn control of yourself over to God.

Well shoot, I wanted to be able to do this on my own. Can't I have just one thing, God, one thing I can claim as my own? I mean, the word self is even in self-discipline. Nope. Okay, great.

This goes back to all of the days before this one and all of the days after this one in this book. They're beautifully interconnected. Self-discipline isn't achieved without God. It's achieved with the prayer of consistency back on Day 5 last week. It's achieved with the posture of submission. It's achieved with grace and forgiveness and a realization that this is not about anything we can do in our own power. The power of the Spirit of God grants us self-discipline.

The Bible calls us to discipline ourselves, but it never once says, "Hey Danielle, you can do this without God, okay?" OR "Hey Danielle once you achieve self-discipline, then you unlock God's love." It's not a video game. You don't "unlock" new levels. You are loved. God gives us His Spirit.

We bow to His holiness, not our own. And self-discipline comes because we love someone, God, more than ourselves.

Discussion Question:

In what ways have you tried to achieve self-discipline in your life?

How'd that go?

Day 5
Habits

1 Corinthians 10:13 (ESV)

No temptation has overtaken you that is not common to man. God is faithful, and he will not let you be tempted beyond your ability, but with the temptation he will also provide the way of escape, that you may be able to endure it.

This is one of the most misconstrued verses in modern day. I see it constantly…. "God will only give me what I can handle" Nope, stop right there. I mean it. That fun little mantra is nowhere to be found in the Bible. What it does say is that God will not let you be tempted beyond your ability and He will always provide you with a way of escaping the temptation. I feel like I'm starting to sound like a broken record here, but I guess if that's to be my plight in life then so be it. If God only gave you what you can handle, you wouldn't need Him. And hopefully by now we've come to an agreement that you and I do in fact need the Lord Jesus Christ.

Let's break it down into the small day to day temptations you are fleeing. Maybe it's gluttony (e.g. raiding the kids' Halloween stash while they're at school), or laziness (e.g. pushing the snooze for the umpteenth million time in the morning), or bitterness e.g. your husband smashes down the trash yet again, instead of just taking it out and you have a whole long argument in your head with him about it, instead of confronting him. (Oh no, that's just me. Okay carry on). Those little habits are temptations. Temptations to pull you back into the mediocre life God did not design for you. By working on resetting some of those habits we can break the chains of temptation. And I'm not here to give you the Sunday school answer either. Some of this is going to take some practical application of the biblical principles of self-control we discussed this week.

But resetting our habit chain works. Let's dissect for just a moment what exactly a habit is. A habit is just a trigger, a response, and a reward. For example, the children are stressing me out (trigger), I reach for a bowl of ice cream (response), ahhhh that's better (reward). But then the cycle starts again. "I shouldn't have eaten that: stress (trigger), more self-sabotaging behavior: the third glass of wine, the second bowl of ice cream, the Netflix binge until 1:00 a.m. (response), ahhhh that's better ... only to have the cycle begin again when the serotonin wears off.

Sisters, we're gonna end this cycle. We're going to lean into Jesus, into His word, and reset those habit chains. It takes recognizing the behaviors going on, and then consistent accountability for leaning into the new habits. But with God we're capable. We can do hard things.

Discussion Questions:

What habit chain do you recognize that you need to change?

Brainstorm some ideas on what new responses you can choose when the trigger happens.

JOURNALING PAGE:

How did your concept of discipline change throughout the week?

_____

_____

_____

_____

_____

_____

_____

_____

_____

_____

_____

_____

_____

_____

_____

_____

_____

Grace Day

Use this day to catch up on any days you might have missed this past week or just spend time lingering with God In your morning process

Figure 2.1

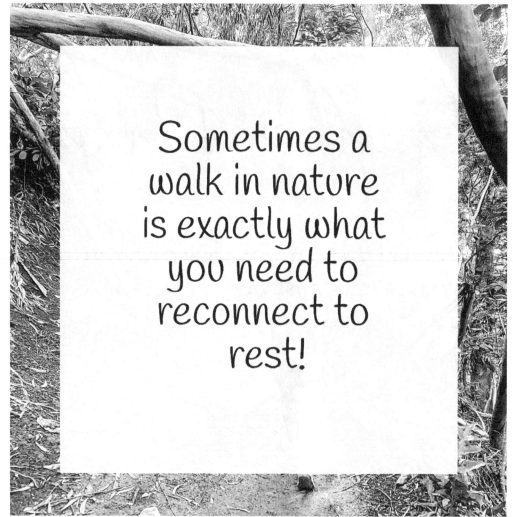

Figure 2.2

Figure 2.3

Recipe – Shaved Brussels Sprouts Salad with Epic Lemon Dressing

Ingredients:
- 1/4 cup olive oil
- 2 Tbsp fresh lemon juice
- 1 1/2 Tbsp nutritional yeast powder
- 1/4 tsp sea salt
- 1/2 tsp black pepper
- 1 pound Brussels sprouts, shaved (thinly sliced or use a mandolin)
- 1/2 cup coarsely chopped dried cherries
- 2 ounces finely grated Parmesan cheese (about 1/2 cup)
- 1/4 cup coarsely chopped fresh flat-leaf parsley
- 1/4 cup pine nuts

Instructions:

Whisk together oil, juice, yeast, salt and pepper in a large serving bowl. Add shaved Brussels sprouts and toss to coat. Let stand at room temperature for 15 minutes. Stir in cherries, cheese, and parsley until combined. Sprinkle with pine nuts to serve.

For full color photos and step by step visual instructions please visit www.daniellemporter.com/recipes

Week 3
Idols

Day 1
Making an Idol of Myself

Psalm 73:26 (ESV)

My flesh and my heart may fail, but God is the strength of my heart and my portion forever.

I'm going to fail. Oof… that's hard to say. If you've ever read anything about the Enneagram test, you'll understand this more than those that haven't. I'm a dead split between an 8 & a 3. Pretty much that should tell you, failing, not being good at something, not being able to control all things is pretty much my virtual hell. But as I've grown in my faith and understanding I've come to recognize we weren't built to win on our own. If we were, we wouldn't need God.

There isn't a time where we're going to get so sufficient we can do it on our own. That's not the way God works. We are reliant on Him. And even though everything in my enneagram 8/3 heart wants to rebel against that thought, that is the truth. There isn't Scripture that says you're on your own once you get to a certain point in your journey with God. Trust me, I searched for it.

The moment we think otherwise, we put ourselves back on that throne. We usurp God's supreme reign and put ourselves in that idol place. Which is never what I want for my life, or yours, friend. We aren't meant to figure it all out, we're meant to worship, bring glory, spread the gospel, and deepen our relationship with Him, not ourselves.

In the world you live in it's almost inevitable you're going to hear the message that you are enough, you've always been enough… but you're not. I'm sorry, if you were you wouldn't need God. You could be your own god, therefore an idol. And I've read the Old Testament in depth and idol worship has never ended well for anyone. Every moment of everyday we need God. You, don't define you, God defines you.

Discussion Questions:

Did you get offended here? I did. Lol, if you haven't taken the Enneagram test yet, do that (there's a free version online if you google it). What's your number?

Did it reveal anything about the way you're wired? It doesn't "mean" anything worth wise, but it can be a helpful tool to facilitate better communication and understanding.

In what ways do you make yourself an idol?

Day 2
Making an Idol of My Children or Lack Thereof

Psalm 16:4

Those who run after other gods will suffer more and more. I will not pour out libations of blood to such gods or take up their names on my lips.

Just like making an idol of ourselves, it's gut-punchingly hard when we realize we make an idol of our children so easily. And y'all, it's so easy. I see it all the time. You post a cutie photo of your precious baby on Insta with the caption "my whole world." Oh friend.

When I became a mom, the world told me that if I didn't give up everything: myself, my husband, my career, all of it for my kids, I wasn't a "good" mom. So I did it. I focused all of my energy on that sweet baby boy. I wanted to give him the whole world. I wanted him to be my world. And it was so easy. I was so highly praised by my friends, family members, and strangers on the internet for what a good mama I was.

What I didn't see was that I lost who God created me to be, and I put that baby above God. Ouch, ouch, ouch.

And with trepidation as I write these words, I watched friends desperate for a baby give up God in pursuit of that child. They held God's love for ransom, "If God loves me, He'll give me a baby," If God loves me, He'll give me a healthy baby. If God loves me, He'll make this child _____ (fill in the blank here, friends). I've watched dear friends suffer miscarriage after miscarriage until that became their story. Until that became their identity. It's heartbreaking. But it's just as heartbreaking to see friends (and myself at one point) be defined by motherhood.

Yes, God loves you. God loves your baby. Our lives and the lives of our children absolutely have purpose, but there's a kingdom-sized eternal perspective that we don't have at an individual level. Which is so hard to hear when we want to be the point. When we want something so badly. But I go back to what I said in yesterday's passage. If we are the point, if our perspective is all that matters, then we don't need God. And if we don't need God, then what's the point?

Motherhood, or lack thereof, does not define you. It is not your identity.

Discussion Questions:

Does this resonate or irritate? I know the first time I heard it, spoken by a dear, dear friend, it hurt. It offended and caused me to go on the defensive.

Do you see this in your own life?

Day 3
Making an Idol of My Career

Jonah 2:8

Those who cling to worthless idols turn away from God's love for them.

Funny enough, I see a whole lot less of this in women than I do in men. My husband is in the Army, and if there's one thing the Army is really good at, it's making you feel like they're the only game in town. If you end your career or service with them then who are you really? A few years ago there came a point in time when we thought my husband's Army career was about done. And identity issues began to crop up. He's been in the military since he was twenty-one years old. And while this is a noble cause, it is not his identity. He had to begin to wrestle with that, and God revealed some idols in his life related to his career.

I watched, thinking this wasn't an issue for me, which is funny, because God was working on my heart as Mat worked through this. As a nutrition counselor and health coach, I never realized this would be an issue for me. Until I didn't hit some goals I had set for my business. Ohhhh lordy, here it came. The self-loathing, the feelings of inadequacy, the bummedness I let it cause me. It's hard to admit, but those feelings are indications that I'm making an idol of the wrong thing. I'm Danielle the girl who's been coaching "this long" and hasn't hit the markers I wanted to hit. And I let it define me… uh oh.

Do you have a spot like that? Where you let the highs & lows of your career define you? Maybe you're on the opposite end of this. Maybe you hit the makers, maybe you shattered the records, maybe you made the millions, maybe you created the thing…. And it consumes you. How can you out-do it next year. It keeps you up at night, you can't rest because you've got to do more, be more, hit bigger markers. Friend, that's an idol too.

Your achievement, or lack thereof in your career does not define you. It is not your identity. Your current career or lack thereof doesn't define you.

Maybe you've seen a theme this week. But none of this defines you. You are defined; your worth rests in your Father, your heavenly Father. It transcends your current circumstances. Whether you're riding your career high, maybe you're jobless, maybe you're rockin' that stay-at-home mom gig… it does not define you. Your relationship with Christ defines you.

Discussion Questions:

Is this something that resonates with you?

Have you ever made an idol of your career or lack thereof?

What indicators do you see that mark that something might be an idol?

Day 4
Making an Idol of Perfection

James 4:6

But he gives us more grace. That is why Scripture says: "God opposes the proud but shows favor to the humble."

"Perfection might seem like the highest calling, but it actually leads to inaction and lack of creativity. Perfectionism is a self-destructive and addictive belief system that fuels the primary thought that if I look perfect and do everything perfectly, I can avoid or minimize the painful feelings of shame, judgment and blame.[1]" - Brené Brown

When we are afraid of making mistakes and looking like we're not perfect, we spend so much time and energy on keeping up the act that we don't have the time or energy to actually live the life God designed for us.

The idolatry of perfection is just a pseudonym for pride.

There was a time in my life where I claimed to be a perfectionist. I did silly things like alphabetize my spice rack and scrub my refrigerator door seal with a toothbrush. I allowed it to stop me from doing so many things. I know it stems from a deep-seated belief that "if you can't do something right don't do it at all," but truly I think my struggle started with a misunderstanding of Revelation 3:15. Somewhere along the way I got it into my head that there were extremes, hot for Christ or cold against Christ, and all I knew is that I didn't want to be in the middle. The result was a perfectionist mindset. If I couldn't be all in all the time on something then I dang sure didn't want to be in the middle, so why do it at all.

---

[1]Brown, Brené. *The Gifts of Imprefection: Let Go of Who You Think You're Supposed to Be and Embrace Who You Are.* Danvers, MA: Hazelden Publishing, 2010.

Growth and maturity are a beautiful thing, and what I found along the way was that the danger of lukewarmness applies to our belief in Jesus Christ and that's about it. You either are for him or you're against him. There is no fence sitting. But that doesn't apply to all of the rest of everything.

So my encouragement here, friend, is to stop waving your perfectionist flag and being proud of it. "Well I'm just a perfectionist so I know if I can't do it perfectly I shouldn't even begin." Not true. Just pick up the Bible and start reading. So what if you aren't going to be perfect with it. Just do five minutes of the workout. Just eat one salad instead of a bag of chips. It's not about checking every box. That's legalism. That's the opposite of the gospel.

Discussion question:

Is this something you struggle with?

Does replacing "perfectionism" with pride change your perspective on it at all?

If it is something you've struggled with, what can you move forward with today, knowing full well perfection isn't the goal?

Day 5
Making an Idol of Anxiety

Philippians 4:6-7

Do not be anxious about anything, but in every situation, by prayer and petition, with thanksgiving, present your requests to God. And the peace of God, which transcends all understanding, will guard your hearts and your minds in Christ Jesus.

As I'm sitting here on a flight direct from Boston to Honolulu, 40,000 feet in the air, I'm surrounded by people marked with anxiety. Anxiety is the number one mental health disorder of 2019, and if the population of this airplane is any indication, the stats are real. But humor me for a moment. Does your worry and anxiousness help the plane fly straighter? Does it keep the plane from crashing? If the pilot heard that someone on board was anxious would that help him fly "better"? I realize these questions are silly, but truly the anxiousness produces nothing but more anxiousness.

Our society has made an idol of anxiety. I'm not denying the chemical imbalance that occurs causing heart racing panic attacks. But I am saying that we have a lot of power in controlling our anxiousness both with the physical world we live in, and the spiritual world we believe in.

The first step is deciding that anxiety has no power over you. This means you have to let go of it as a crutch. And trust me, I get gaggy even writing this because I know the backlash that will occur when the people I currently know read my beliefs and experiences in this subject. But the truth is just like any other story we've decided is our identity. Anxiety provides "accidental benefits" we may actually enjoy a little too much.

Hear me out. When we break a leg and are given actual crutches from the hospital, we have to rely on them to get around. But even those crutches produce some "accidental benefits." Things such as when people hold the door, carry your things, or are overly accommodating. I'm not saying you'd trade your mobility and independence for this permanently, but there is definitely a way to enjoy the benefits a little too much. Stay on the crutches when it's convenient for you. But when no one is around, you exercise your independence. It's the same when you cling to the identity of being broke. "Oh, I can't go out. I'm broke." The accidental benefit? "Don't worry friend, we've got your dinner tonight."

Anxiety is no different. When we allow it to become our story, not just something we have (like any other disease or disorder) we receive the accidental benefits and sometimes enjoy them a little too much. For example, when there's an event you don't want to go to, a person you don't want to be around, a meeting you can't take, or using it as a reason for your tardiness.

The thing is, though, that when the anxiety becomes your identity, you've made it an idol, and just like any other idol, God calls it sin.

Mark 4:18-19 shows us God wants his children marked by peace, and our constant idolatry of anxiousness is a bad testimony to God's all-powerful nature.

I am in no way condemning anyone for having anxiety or battling anxious moments. But I do ask that you place this at the feet of Jesus and ask the Holy Spirit to convict you if needed.

So what do we do here? How do we battle making an idol of anxiety? Just as with everything else, Scripture is our guide. Philippians 4:6-7 tells us what to do, how to do it and what to expect. But it's not enough just to read Scripture. It's not a magic spell. It works just as well as reading a cookbook fills your belly. If anything, reading a cookbook can cause an even deeper hunger. You've got to put Scripture into practice over and over in order to combat the lies of the enemy.

Your anxiety does not define you. It does not have to be the end of your story. You, with the power of the Holy Spirit living in you, have the power to banish it in the name of the Savior. And remember there is obviously medical causes for anxiety that need to be addressed with your doctor or a counseling professional. Please don't fear getting help. God gifted many professionals with tools that can help you. But just like with many other medical conditions there are lifestyle changes that can occur that will ease symptoms and aid in medical intervention.

Discussion Questions:

Is anxiety something you've battled in the past?

What was your approach before?

Is there something in the Philippians passage you can put into action today?

JOURNALING PAGE:

How did your perspective of idolatry change throughout the week?

_____

_____

_____

_____

_____

_____

_____

_____

_____

_____

_____

_____

_____

_____

_____

_____

_____

_____

_____

Grace Day

Use this day to catch up on any days you might
have missed this past week or just spend time
lingering with God In your morning process

Figure 3.1

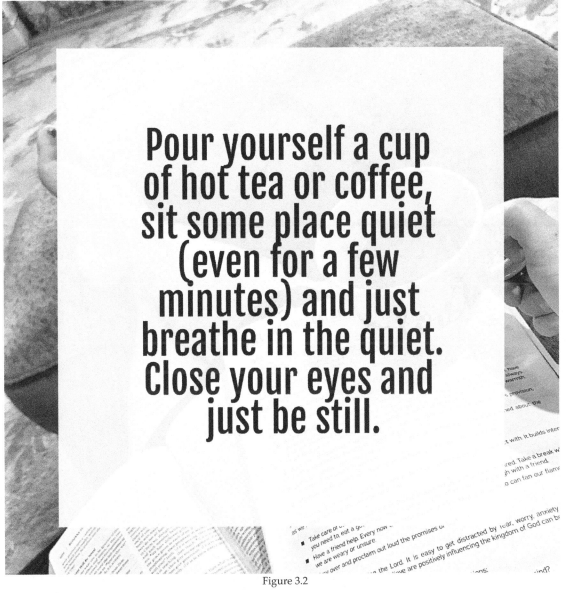

Pour yourself a cup of hot tea or coffee, sit some place quiet (even for a few minutes) and just breathe in the quiet. Close your eyes and just be still.

Figure 3.2

Figure 3.3

56

Recipe: Chopped Chicken and Broccoli Apple Slaw

INGREDIENTS:

- 2 tsp Avocado Oil Mayonnaise
- 2 tbsp apple cider vinegar
- 1 tsp Dijon mustard
- Salt & Pepper to taste
- 1 (13oz bag) broccoli slaw, approx. 3 cups
- 1 small apple sliced into matchstick sized pieces
- 1/3 cup chopped cook chicken breast, approx. 2 oz
- ¼ medium red onion, sliced thin
- 1 large hard-boiled egg, chopped

INSTRUCTIONS:

1) To make dressing, combine mayo, vinegar & mustard in a medium bowl. Season with salt and pepper if desired. Whisk to blend, set aside.
2) Combine broccoli slaw, apple, chicken and onion in a medium serving bowl. Toss gently to blend.
3) Drizzle with dressing. Toss gently together to blend.
4) Place sliced hard-boiled egg on top. Serve immediately.

For full color photos and step by step visual instructions please visit www.daniellemporter.com/recipes

Part 2
Using Our Bodies to Glorify God

Week 4
Practical Application

Day 1
Prayer

Jeremiah 29:12 (ESV)

Then you will call upon me and come and pray to me, and I will hear you.

Prayer is one of those things I can't remember NOT doing. I mean from birth we prayed over every meal, every bedtime, every church service. But it wasn't until I learned more about meditation that I really started to understand prayer on a deeper level.

Prayer isn't just saying a memorized group of words because that's the way your family has always prayed. Jesus reminds us in Matthew 6 to not babble on in vain. This is a time for you to talk to your heavenly Father. It's silencing your squirrel brain and focusing on communing with God. And thankfully Jesus gives us a structure to follow, so we don't end up just babbling and repeating the same words mindlessly. Matthew 6 reminds us that it should include thanks-giving, interceding on another's behalf, asking for forgiveness, and asking for what the Holy Spirit has laid on your heart to ask, but it's also got to include silence. It's got to include some time to just listen. This is hard. I completely understand that. But if God's going to speak back, you've got to be listening. God speaks all throughout the day in all different ways: through nature, experiences, His Word, through wise people, but also in your prayer life.

One of the ways I've worked on quieting my squirrel brain is through a breathing technique I learned from my husband's military friends. It's a breath counting exercise that pulls your focus to your breath, so you can listen and truly hear. Start by closing your eyes and inhaling for a count of five slowly. Then hold the breath for a count of five, then slowly exhale for a count of five. Keep doing this until your mind becomes quiet. Usually, I can do about two to five minutes of this before my focus is completely gone, but praise God for the two to five minutes where my big yap is quiet.

Discussion Question:

Try this breathing exercise.
How long did you make it?

Are you going to keep practicing?

Did you hear God speak in your silence?

Day 2
Visualization

Romans 8:24-25

For in this hope we were saved. But hope that is seen is no hope at all. Who hopes for what they already have? But if we hope for what we do not yet have, we wait for it patiently.

Talk to any successful person and they will tell you they visualize the successful outcome before it happens. Whether in sports (visualizing the game winning shot) or business (visualizing how the deal will go down) or really anything, they're all visualizing how it's going to go down.

We do have to address the difference between visualizing as a Christian who believes God directs our steps and visualizing as a non-believer who believes they are in control of all the steps. Just like in Proverbs where Solomon writes to commit to the Lord whatever you do, that's not just for pastors and people doing Christiany things. It's for smacking the game-winning ball high up over the fence. It's for the CEO who's closing a business deal. It's for mamas leading their children. It's for everyone.

And remember God gifts us the ability to hear his promptings, so your hopes and dreams can be nudges from God. So don't be afraid to pray and ask God for his will and wisdom when it comes to your desires. Your vision for how God will use you is valuable. It may not turn out the way you pictured it, but when your heart is to glorify God in that you do, big things can absolutely happen.

So spending a little time each day visualizing how your day will go will only bring more glory to God. Visualize yourself greeting your children as they wake up. Visualize yourself happily making their breakfast as they chatter to you about their dreams. Visualize yourself glorifying God all through the day before it even starts. Visualize the ways throughout the day you'll serve Him. Visualize your husband stepping up to be the Christ centered head of your household.

We are so blessed to be a part of God's plan. He does not need us, He wants us. I want to be the version of Danielle that dwells on glorifying God before the other demands of the day get in the way.

Discussion Question:

Have you ever "visualized" before?

How did that change the way you experienced your day?

If you haven't, give visualization a try. See if it changes anything.

Day 3
Exercise

Romans 12:1

Therefore, I urge you, brothers and sisters, in view of God's mercy, to offer your bodies as a living sacrifice, holy and pleasing to God—this is your true and proper worship.

Life in the New Testament was understandably different from life in 2020, as I'm sitting in my living room on my laptop writing this book. Prior to the industrial revolution there really wasn't much reason for exercise like we have now. Life itself was exercise. You woke up and tilled and planted and harvested and walked to get water and your whole day, unless you were the queen of England, had some physical activity until you crashed into your hay bale bed at sundown. Obesity just wasn't a common occurrence. Obesity was a sign of affluence. You had the time to not work and sweat and toil. So let's be real clear here. God is the God of then and the God of now, so He isn't speaking through Paul to the Romans about running on a treadmill as being a living sacrifice.

But as we discuss a lot in this book, God created our bodies to live in harmony with Him and with the Earth He created. One of the ways we live a whole and nourished life is to move our bodies. God made our bodies to move! The way my hyper-logical brain works is in opposites. If God made our bodies to be sedentary then we would function best that way, which we know isn't true. Because what happens when you lay down or sit down for too long? Our bodies begin to shut down. Our muscles atrophy, and our metabolism slows because we aren't using energy. So if logic tells us that's not the way we should live, and we don't currently live in an agricultural setting, exercise it is, friend.

The type of exercise is not all that important, honestly. It's that you got up, did it, moved your body, got your heart rate up and your blood flowing before the rest of the day happens. Because if you're anything like me, if you put it off until the afternoon, or the kids' nap time or even worse, after dinner, it will never happen.

So why not reframe the mindset around that time to be one of worshipping God. Moving the body he gave us as an act of worship. To express gratitude for the breath in our lungs and the muscles that move!

For me that ended up being at-home workouts. I just couldn't get myself consistently out the door to the gym when I had small children. Plus I couldn't justify the time expended driving there and back and waiting for equipment etc. But if you're a gym girl, then go for it. If you want to run, then get out there and pound that pavement.

But do something active before life begins to demand your time and frame it as an act of worship and time with the Lord.

Discussion questions:

Have you ever considered exercise as an act of worship?

What kind of exercise do you do now?

If none, would you consider making a commitment to add even five minutes of stretching into your morning routine?

Day 4
Gratitude

Colossians 1:12

and giving joyful thanks to the Father, who has qualified you to share in the inheritance of his holy people in the kingdom of light.

Of all the aspects of my daily practice, gratitude might be my favorite. They all deserve their place of honor, but expressing gratitude changes everything. It impacts every other aspect of life in such a beautiful, life-giving way.

On a practical level for me, this became more of just expressing gratitude through prayer. It's easier in your prayer to say "thank you God for ___" than it is to take the time to write it down, but having a gratitude journal has had such an impact in my life. It forces me to focus on what I'm grateful for rather than all the woes and problems in my life. Plus, having a written account gives you physical evidence of the good and gracious things God has given you. Because I promise there will be days when gratitude is hard. When life is just all lemons and you need that reminder of the ways God has blessed you.

A gratitude practice sounds like a new-agey, positive-psychology sounding kind of thing, but just like many secular things, they find their root in the Bible. Again, we find an act of worship in our morning routine. Worshipping God through recalling His goodness from the previous day sets us up to focus on the things to be grateful for in this current day. You don't have to spend all morning doing this but take just a few minutes every morning to write down three things you're grateful for. Try not to be repetitive, but truly consider the previous days and what light is shining from them. And I call it a practice because it does take practice. Especially when days don't seem so bright and it takes intentional practice to find the things to be grateful for.

Gratitude transforms you from the inside out. Grateful people have a special glow about them; they're intentionally seeking God's goodness in every day.

Discussion Questions:

Do you keep a gratitude journal?

Is intentional gratitude something you've invested any part of your day in before?

My challenge to you is to keep a gratitude journal for the next week and see if it begins to impact your life in a positive way.

Day 5
Scripture

Romans 15:4 (ESV)

For whatever was written in former days was written for our instruction, that through endurance and through the encouragement of the Scriptures we might have hope.

The last step in our morning practice is Scripture. And not just Scripture for Scripture's sake, to check a box and claim you "did" your Scripture reading for the day. I mean Scripture for affirmation sake. We need to affirm the promises of God, to hide them in our hearts. Scripture commands us to use the sword of the spirit, Ephesians 6: 10-18. I found that when I neglected affirming scripture, I handed the enemy the microphone in my mind. Truth cards were my way of reclaiming that space. When Satan starts spewing lies, the best and only effective way of reclaiming the microphone is to hold up a truth card, reminding Satan that he has no claim here.

If you go to www.daniellemporter.com, you can download your own set of truth cards for free. These cards were designed to be the practical application for Ephesians 6:17. Because remember, the serpent didn't come to Eve asking her to lie, kill and destroy. He came to her simply questioning the word of God. With these truth cards you can push back the enemy's simple questions about who you are, who God made you to be, and combat the lies that can start to sound true if you don't hide the word of God in your heart.

Ephesians 6:13-16 is our defense, "Therefore put on the full armor of God, so that when the day of evil comes, you may be able to stand your ground, and after you have done everything, to stand. Stand firm then, with the belt of truth buckled around your waist, with the breastplate of righteousness in place, and with your feet fitted with the readiness that comes from the gospel of peace. In addition to all this, take up the shield of faith, with which you can extinguish all the flaming arrows of the evil one."

And Ephesians 6:17 is our offense, "Take the helmet of salvation and the sword of the Spirit, which is the word of God." These truth cards are our offense to Satan's lies. Each and every morning I read these promises of God, they begin my day with God's living Word. Not just alive for those in the time it was written, but alive and moving in my life, your life, and the lives around us that we impact.

This is in no way a substitute for any daily Scripture reading, but these cards are affirmations of God's promises for your life. Reading them daily, first thing, will give you a stronger backbone for the rest of the day. There are hundreds of promises in the Bible, the ones on the cards are just some that have truly changed my life when read daily.

Discussion Questions:

Go to www.daniellemporter.com and download the truth cards, print them on cardstock (or you can just rewrite them on index cards) and put them on a clasp so you can have them handy in your morning routine area. These are vital to your morning process. As vital as putting on your underwear and brushing your teeth, let God's word be your battle cry.

JOURNALING PAGE:

How did your development of a morning practice change throughout the week?

_____

_____

_____

_____

_____

_____

_____

_____

_____

_____

_____

_____

_____

_____

_____

_____

_____

_____

_____

_____

_____

Grace Day

Use this day to catch up on any days you might
have missed this past week or just spend time
lingering with God In your morning process

Figure 4.1

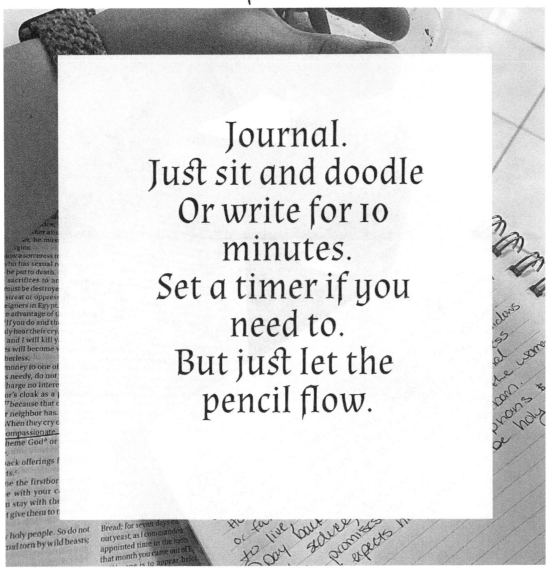

Journal.
Just sit and doodle
Or write for 10
minutes.
Set a timer if you
need to.
But just let the
pencil flow.

Figure 4.2

Figure 4.3

Recipe: Chili Cheese Fries – the healthy way

Ingredients:
Fries:
- 3 small sweet potatoes, spiralized (you can also use frozen good quality sweet potato fries to make this even quicker)
- Salt
- Pepper
- Garlic powder

****You can also use carrot spirals or turnip spirals for a lower carb option****

Skillet Chili:
- 1lb ground turkey
- 1 can reduced sodium kidney beans, rinsed
- 1 can fire-roasted diced tomatoes
- 1 can green chilies (small can)
- 1 red bell pepper, diced
- 1 tsp cumin powder
- 1/2 tsp chili powder
- 1/2 tsp garlic powder
- 1/4 tsp pink Himalayan salt

Optional:
- Cheese (I used Monterey jack)
- Avocado
- Greek yogurt
- Green onions

Directions:

Preheat the oven to 415 degrees.

Start the skillet chili first. This can also be meal prepped days in advance or make a huge batch and freeze it. Brown the ground turkey with seasoning and diced bell pepper. As the turkey is cooking pour in the can of tomatoes, green chilies and rinsed kidney beans (if this mix is getting too dry in the pan put a little of the bean water in there).

While the chili is cooking, put tin foil down on a cookie sheet. Spiralize the sweet potato if it's not already spiralized. If you're using frozen sweet potato fries go ahead and throw them in the oven and get them baking according to the package directions. If you are spiralizing the sweet potato, drizzle the spirals with olive oil, sprinkle with seasonings. Spread them out on the baking sheet. Bake the spirals at 415 for 10 minutes.

When the sweet potatoes are finished pour the chili over top, top with cheese. Crank up the oven to broil. Put the whole baking sheet back in and broil for 7 minutes.

Pull it out and bang, you're eating healthy chili cheese fries!

For full color photos and step by step visual instructions please visit www.daniellemporter.com/recipes

Week 5
Nutrition & Fitness

Day 1
Food as fuel

1 Corinthians 10:31

So whether you eat or drink or whatever you do, do it all for the glory of God.

I've struggled with my weight for most of my life, specifically from about age ten until thirty. As I sit here writing this book, I am thirty-six years old. For twenty years I tried to convince myself that I didn't love food. I dieted, deprived myself of nutrients, ate tasteless cardboard and zero-calorie food. After all, it's just fuel, right? I can suck it up and live on carrot sticks and diet shakes. It's okay if it tastes terrible. It's low calorie and that's all that matters!

Sisters, there is more to food than the calorie count. Your body is made for more than just getting smaller or bigger!

Food is a gift from God. We use it to celebrate, to mourn, to entertain, to fuel, to love, to show hospitality, and to care for people in tangible ways. Yes, there are dangers to overeating (just as there are to under-eating), but we need food on a daily basis.

So in April 2014, when I set out to make lifestyle adjustments to pursue a healthier body, I approached things differently. God gave me a friend who imparted His truth to me. God didn't create manufactured, highly processed, chemically based food. He created vegetables, He created meat, He created fruits, He created grains, He created legumes and seeds and plants. He did not create bags of chips. (Sorry friends, He just didn't.)

When you view food this way, it changes things. When you start recognizing the synergistic way God created your body, your internal digestion system and the way he created whole food to nourish that system, your perspective starts to shift regarding what food does for you.

I get it, at first carrots don't taste as good as chips. But what if I told you it's because you conditioned your taste buds to like Doritos and not carrots? You don't "like" the taste of water. What if I told you scientifically it's because you have conditioned your taste buds that way?

Nourishing your body with primarily (not all, this isn't about legalism!) whole, unprocessed foods will always result in a healthier body. Always. Because God designed it that way back in Genesis.

Discussion Questions:

What do you think of this?

Do you already view food this way or is this something you're looking at shifting in your own life?

Day 2
Fitness

1 Corinthians 9:27 (NKJV)

But I discipline my body and bring it into subjection, lest, when I have preached to others, I myself should become disqualified.

When Mat and I were first looking at names for our business we knew we wanted the name to have a biblical significance. You know, like the egg cartons that have a Bible verse inside (sneaky gospel right there, folks). But we hemmed and hawed back and forth about what verse would speak to the nutrition, fitness, mindset, and resiliency business we wanted to market to the masses. We landed on Paul's letter to the Corinthians where he talks about disciplining his body to bring it into subjection.

Now hear me out. I do not think Paul was out there doing burpees for Jesus. I don't think he was running laps on the track preachin' the gospel. But I do believe he held his body in high regard as an example of what can happen when we let it all go vs when we bring it under submission. Our body and its sinful predisposition to laziness and sloth is the perfect example of long-term consequences resulting from short-term pleasures.

What happens when we forego exercise for Netflix binges for too long? What happens when we ride the elevator everyday rather than take the stairs? What happens when we drive around the parking lot for fifteen minutes rather than parking and walking from the back row? That evidence is visible on our bodies to the tune of increased body fat, low muscle tone, shortness of breath, and lifestyle diseases.

It's no different in our spiritual journey. If all we ever do is take the lazy route… you know what I'm talking about. Going to church, but scrolling Instagram while you're sitting in the pew. Reading our five-minute-for-women devotional while sitting on the toilet in the morning. Those behaviors don't lead to an on-fire heart for Christ. They just don't. It doesn't mean God isn't working, but halfheartedness doesn't lead to full-hearted results. Instead, we give into our fleshly desires rather than leaning into the difficult work of bringing our bodies into submission.

So yes, that does mean I highly value exercise, and stupid, stinkin' burpees. It doesn't mean I like them. But it does mean that those are the things that bring this body into submission. It's not about vanity, it's about temple reconstruction.

Sister, if you've let it all go, there is grace upon grace. But there's also temple restoration work to be done. Find yourself an accountability tribe. if you don't know of one send me an email and we'll get you plugged into mine (nourish927@gmail.com). Do the work. Fight the flesh. Your health is worth the investment. Someone unable to move the way they want, stuck with a preventable disease because of a sedentary lifestyle, can't do all the ministry work God is calling them to do.

Discussion Questions:

Where does fitness fit into your life?

What are some ways you can increase your fitness?

What steps are you going to take next to increase exercise in your life if it needs to be increased?

Day 3
Mindset

Philippians 4:8 (KJV)

Finally, brethren, whatsoever things are true, whatsoever things are honest, whatsoever things are just, whatsoever things are pure, whatsoever things are lovely, whatsoever things are of good report; if there be any virtue, and if there be any praise, think on these things.

The things we focus on are what we see. My favorite example of this is the game my kids and I play: "banana car." My children and I search for yellow cars. And when we find one, we shout out "banana car." it gives us something to do in the car other than fuss at one another. Ha ha. When we first started this game, we picked yellow because it's a seemingly uncommon car color. But all of the sudden when we started searching for them, they were everywhere. Years later I'm still shouting "banana car" every time I see one. It's like that with everything. What we focus on becomes what we see. So if you start searching out the positive, the beautiful, the God moments … guess what you see everywhere. You see the good, the beautiful, the lovely. You see God everywhere.

I grew up a cynic. I was raised to look at the negatives in everything. As soon as an opportunity presented itself, I could easily come up with ten reasons it wouldn't work. It's a trait I have to actively combat in my life. I had to start intentionally searching out all of the positives. Paul tells us in Philippians to dwell on those things that are honest, just, pure and lovely. What do you think would happen if you started intentionally finding things to thank God for? What would happen if you started spending your day finding bright spots? Guess what? You'd barely see the darkness anymore.

In the same vein, when we focus on all of our downfalls and sins and ways we don't measure up it's all we can see. What if instead you focused on who God says you are? Instead of focusing on the weight you need to lose, or the flab on your arms, or the wrinkles developing around your mouth… you choose to intentionally focus on how God wants you to nourish your body, the hugs you can give and on the smiles those creases came from.

Just like if you stare at a candle in a dark room, your eyes adjust. Let's adjust our eyes to see what God wants us to see.

Discussion questions:

Back on Day 4 of Week 3 I asked you to keep a gratitude journal. Is that something you've continued doing?

If so, how has it changed your perspective?

Where else can you shift your perspective?

Day 4
How they all work together

1 Corinthians 6:19-20 (ESV)

Or do you not know that your body is a temple of the Holy Spirit within you, whom you have from God? You are not your own, for you were bought with a price. So glorify God in your body.

What does it mean to be a wholly healthy person? Not a holy, healthy person, because only God can make you holy, but wholly – meaning whole. God designed the parts of our whole body to work synergistically together. Not to work as a bunch of parts to be tinkered with independently. When we embark on a whole health journey, it has to include working on our nutrition, fitness, and mindset.

My way to explain this is that it is my deep and sincere belief that we cannot be the most effective in God's kingdom if we aren't working on being wholly healthy. I've sat slack jawed listening to well-meaning Christians proclaim that what we eat doesn't matter to God; that what matters is our testimony and how we share Christ with others. Ummmm . . . pardon?!

Now I'll agree that when we let food or fitness, or anything for that matter, consume our thoughts, we aren't effective witnesses for Christ (actually if we do that, we're making idols, which last time I checked is a big no no). But I will not agree that it doesn't matter. Sharing the gospel is difficult when we're consumed with preventable lifestyle diseases or when we've depleted every ounce of mental energy we have serving our children. It's hard to share the gospel when we can barely speak after ascending a staircase. I'm not saying you can't. You can preach from a hospital bed for goodness' sake. But I am asking, is that what God made you for? Did God make you to tear down the temple He gave you?

Mindset, nutrition, and fitness are the trifecta of whole health. If you're too depressed to function, it doesn't matter if you can do 1000 burpees. And vice versa if you're carrying so much extra body weight you're not able to breathe by the time you hit the top of the stairs. It doesn't matter if you are calm and at peace in your mind if you can't breathe!

God created us on purpose for a purpose. If we aren't attending to those three pieces of the puzzle the wholeness will always been lopsided, making it easy for idols to come in.

Discussion Question:

Where have you seen this played out? Has this been an issue in your life?

Day 5
Resiliency

Romans 8:37 (ESV)

No, in all these things we are more than conquerors through him who loved us.

Mat has always had a dream of opening a resiliency center. A place where people can go to learn skills that help build resiliency. A place where fitness, nutrition, mental health counseling, and spiritual counseling exist in one place. I think our time in the military life has shown him the true value of resiliency. All the constant moving, wars, deployments, etc., weighs on a person.

I think it's important to look at what resiliency looks like in real life. I always picture it as a rubber band. It can be stretched beyond what you can possibly imagine and always snap back into shape. Until it doesn't. Until it rots and then even the slightest pull breaks it. I think of us like that. We take it all in and bounce back over and over… until we don't. Until the slightest thing makes us snap. But the rubber band didn't just disintegrate. Outside forces and elements caused the disintegration.

Everything we're talking about here in this book is a stepping-stone to a better sense of resiliency. And it takes all of it in varying degrees to shape a person marked by resiliency. Fitness, nutrition, mindset, personal responsibility, and constant dependency on Christ … it all rolls into a more healthy, whole, resilient person. The Bible reminds us we aren't complete until eternity or Christ's return (whichever comes first), but while we're here, on this Earth, resiliency will shape our perspective.

Each steppingstone on your way to a whole and nourished life involves a piece of you. First, map out on the Wheel of Life where you are now on a scale of 1–10 (10 being highest) in each area of your life. You have to take a good honest look at where you are before you can begin any kind of improvement. Often when people embark on improving their life, they focus heavily on one specific area, but placing all of your effort on one area typically ends up with a lopsided wheel.

What is one thing you can do today to work on smoothing out the bumpy ride?

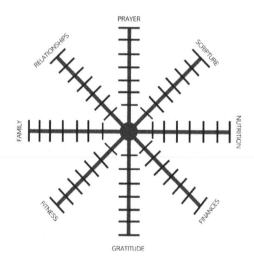

Figure 5.1

Discussion Question:

Would you characterize yourself as resilient?

If not, what part of your "wheel of life" would you say is lopsided?

What practical "today" kinda thing can you do to help it roll along more smoothly?

JOURNALING PAGE:

How did your concept of the way God views your body shift throughout the week?

_____

_____

_____

_____

_____

_____

_____

_____

_____

_____

_____

_____

_____

_____

_____

_____

_____

_____

Grace Day

Use this day to catch up on any days you might
have missed this past week or just spend time
lingering with God In your morning process

Figure 5.2

Can you take a nap today? It doesn't have to be long, but can you find a few minutes for a short little snooze?

Figure 5.3

Figure 5.4

Recipe – Lazy Girl Breakfast Casserole

INGREDIENTS:

- Five generous servings of vegetables – diced (I used onion, mini bell pepper and spinach) (other options, zucchini or broccoli)
- 4 links of Nitrate free chicken sausage (I used chicken, spinach & asiago sausage)
- Frozen spinach
- 12 eggs (preferably free range, cage free)
- 4 tablespoons of ghee (can substitute butter)
- Bagel Seasoning
- salt and pepper to taste

DIRECTIONS:

1. Pre-heat oven to 350 degrees
2. Grease bottom of 13x9 glass dish with butter
3. Place frozen spinach, diced veggies & sausage in bottom of a 13x9 Pyrex baking dish
4. In a large bowl, crack and beat the 12 eggs.
5. Pour over veggies & Sausage
6. Bake at 350 degrees for 30 minutes or until casserole turns golden on the edges.
7. Slice into 8 equal pieces

For full color photos and step by step visual instructions please visit www.daniellemporter.com/recipes

Week 6
Freedom

Day 1
The Freedom Ride

Galatians 5:7

You were running a good race. Who cut in on you to keep you from obeying the truth?

I'm a super visual learner; the more word pictures the better in my opinion. So go with me here… There's this horse … we'll call him Liberty. He's got a rider, you perhaps. The horse is racing toward freedom, true, abundant freedom in Christ. But there are two directions most riders can fall off.

The rider can fall off on the side of legalism, which is what we have here with slavery. Being shackled to a set of rules, even good ones, but shackled to them for the wrong purpose is still slavery. We go more into the connection between legalism and slavery this week, but in summary, Paul is reminding the former Jews of their yoke of burden prior to Jesus. There were up to 613 Jewish commandments to keep in order to fulfill the Law of Moses. Bondage to the law created the disconnect that was the ultimate downfall of the Pharisees. Legalism never works.

Or the rider can fall off in the other direction, license. They say, okay, freedom means I get to do whatever I want with no consequence because Jesus paid it all. Either way you're falling off the horse. Grace is what keeps us upright when we want start to lean.

So if the goal here is to stay on the horse, Liberty, we need to know the pitfalls on either side so we aren't tempted like the Galatians to fall prey to the traps of legalism or license.

Discussion Question:

What does freedom in Christ look like to you?

Do you typically lean to one side or the other legalism or license?

Day 2
Slavery = Legalism

Galatians 5:1

It is for freedom that Christ has set us free. Stand firm, then, and do not let yourselves be burdened again by a yoke of slavery.

Slavery is such a strong word. Immediately when I think of slavery because of my upbringing south of the Mason Dixon Line, I think of pre-civil war American slavery, a heavy and harsh topic. But Paul uses it here to remind the new Christians who were former Jews, of the slavery God brought them out of in Egypt. They were burdened, torn down, and oppressed. God raised them up, even though they didn't deserve it, and set them on a freedom path.

Why then can't I consider the legalism I try to strap on my shoulders slavery? That's what it is. God + anything is slavery. So God plus obligation to church traditions = slavery. God plus eating a certain way = slavery. God plus this specific weekly regimen = slavery.

Connecting the dots to your physical health journey, legalism rarely works for long. If there's anything I learned in my cycle of perpetual dieting, the tighter I tried to tighten the reigns, lock it down with laws, the higher my weight went. Research shows that when you participate in restrictive diets, any weight that you lose will come back plus 15% when you quit the diet. The same is paralleled in our spiritual life when we, like the Jews try to the letter of the law, we will fail.

While we were created to crave boundaries, we also we created to crave freedom. God tells us the freedom exists when the spirit of the boundary is understood.

Human instinct craves boundaries; God placed boundaries on us from day one. It's in our blood! We see a similar situation with children. We desperately want them to obey the boundaries, but not for just blind obedience's sake. We want them to understand that boundaries equal love. We love them enough to shield them from small things that might lead to big problems.

And that's how God works with us. He shows us that it's not just about the rule, it's the spirit in which the rule was created. He loves us enough to protect us. Strapping ourselves to the yoke of box-checking obedience isn't stirring our soul. Box-checking isn't enough.

Discussion Questions:

What legalism trap do you fall in most often?

What are the boxes you start mindlessly checking off in your pursuit for a more nourished life?

Day 3
License

Galatians 5:13

You, my brothers and sisters, were called to be free. But do not use your freedom to indulge the flesh; rather, serve one another humbly in love.

So if we're leaning really hard to the opposite side of legalism, what can that look like? For most, it's license. You can do whatever you want, whenever you want, however you want … because grace baybay! WOOO! Ehhh, slow your roll there thriller. Yes, grace covers all things, but that doesn't mean it's beneficial for the kingdom of God, or for you either, to throw out all the rules and live however you want. I love what Paul says in 1 Corinthians 6 about all things being permissible but not all things being beneficial. For visual effect sake we'll go back to food here. Just because you can eat whatever you want in whatever quantity you want doesn't mean you should eat whatever you want in whatever quantity you want. Even someone who is visually healthy doesn't need six bags of chips. Our bodies were beautifully designed to be fueled in a wonderful way and when you overfill the tank, we're not better for it.

Going back to our health. License doesn't work there either. Connecting the dots between the physical and spiritual has always been the point of this devotional. You don't just get to give up caring about what you put in your body because you accepted Christ and your glorified body is waiting in Heaven. God cares about you now too.

It's easy to believe that because of salvation, Christians can do whatever we want. But that's not true. If you love someone you don't treat them like garbage. It's not for fear they'll stop loving you, it's because you love them, and you want to treat them well because you love them. You want to honor your spouse because you love him, not because if you don't he'll punish you or because it doesn't matter since he'll forgive you anyway. No! So how much more can we show our love for God, who saved us from eternal damnation, than by obedience?

Discussion Questions:

Be honest, do you get tripped up by legalism or license more?

Have you experienced license in your own life with either your physical health or spiritual journey?

Day 4
Free Indeed

John 8:36

If the Son sets you free, you will be free indeed.

There's a difference between being free, and being free indeed. I once heard a story that illuminated this difference perfectly for me and I'm desperate to share it with you.

You see, there were two prisoners in jail. One planned an elaborate escape, tunneled out and ran like a dog unleashed. He was free. The other prisoner served his time, completed his sentence and on his release date was set free. He was free. Which one was free indeed? Obviously the second man, right? The first will never stop looking behind him, even if he runs, swims, and flies as far as he can, he'll never stop flinching at siren sounds. He'll never be truly free because his price wasn't paid. The second man's price was paid, he served his time, and was set free. He will never serve that sentence again. He is free indeed.

Sisters, that's what Christ offers us: a price paid, a sentence served. Undeserved, unworthy grace resulting in abounding freedom. We simply have to accept it.

Our chains can be broken, but only by the Chain Breaker. We can run from our bad habits, we can behavior-modify all kinds of things, but Jesus is the only one who can ever truly set us free. His freedom is eternal. The freedom we manufacture can always be taken away. But we can walk in the freedom of a life set free. One where we lay our burdens at His feet and never ever pick them up again. Why, friends, do we continue to pick up the same burdens over and over? Christ has set us free. Now it's up to us to walk in that freedom. That comes from daily surrender.

Discussion questions:

Have you accepted God's grace & freedom?

If not, what holds you back?

Day 5
God of Transformation

2 Corinthians 5:17 (ESV)

Therefore, if anyone is in Christ, he is a new creation. The old has passed away; behold, the new has come.

Transformation is happening all around us. One quick Instagram hashtag search and you can see hundreds of thousands of physical weight loss transformations and it's easy to believe we can just will ourselves there. That we can buckle down, do all the steps, and boom, true and lasting transformation is there. But that's not reality.

Our God is a God of true transformation. Not just a little weight loss, or a new morning routine, or breaking the chains of addiction, but everlasting, eternal transformation. That transformation happens from the inside out. My story is one I've labeled as "A Nourished Life" not because I lost 100 pounds, and not because I am actively working to break a family legacy of addiction, shame, self-deprecation and low body image. I now live a nourished life because of the new creation God has created me to be. He always transforms us before He transforms our circumstances.

My external transformation only has meaning because of the spiritual, internal transformation. Without that, it's just a nice "after" photo. I invite you to not only pursue a great morning routine, some healthy habits, and a new attitude, but to pursue righteousness, pursue sanctification, and pursue true and total everlasting and eternal transformation.

Discussion Questions:

What in your life has transformed in the last six weeks?

Where do you need to pursue transformation?

JOURNALING PAGE:

How have you experienced growth throughout the week in regards to the true transformation God offers?

_____

_____

_____

_____

_____

_____

_____

_____

_____

_____

_____

_____

_____

_____

_____

_____

_____

_____

_____

_____

Grace Day

Use this day to catch up on any days you might have missed this past week or just spend time lingering with God In your morning process

Figure 6.1

Turn on some worship music & throw those hands in the air, friend. Worship the King of Kings!

Figure 6.2

Figure 6.3

116

Recipe: Gluten-free Pumpkin Apple Bread

INGREDIENTS
- 3 cups gluten-free flour
- 2 tablespoons coconut flour
- 1 tablespoon pumpkin pie spice
- 2 teaspoons baking soda
- 1 1/2 teaspoon salt
- 1 1/2 cups coconut sugar
- 1/2 cup maple syrup
- 1: 15 ounce can pumpkin puree
- 4 large eggs
- 1/2 cup melted coconut oil
- 1/2 cup 0% plain Greek yogurt
- 2 cups diced apples, cored

INSTRUCTIONS
1. Preheat oven to 375 degrees Fahrenheit and grease two 9x5-inch loaf pans (OR 1 loaf pan and 1 muffin tin) w/ coconut oil & gf flour.
2. In a large bowl, whisk together the dry ingredients. Set aside.
3. In the bowl of a stand mixer, add syrup, pumpkin puree, eggs, coconut oil, and Greek yogurt. Beat together on low speed.
4. Carefully add the dry mixture in batches to the wet ingredients and mix until just combined.
5. Add the diced apples to the mixture and fold in with a spatula.
6. Evenly divide the batter amongst the two greased loaf pans and smooth out the tops.
7. OR divide between loaf pan and muffin pan.
8. Bake for 60-75 minutes, or until a toothpick stuck in the center comes out clean. If you are using the muffin tin, begin checking muffins with toothpick at 25 minutes.
9. Let cool completely then place on a wire rack to finish cooling to room temperature.
10. At this point you can slice up the bread or you can wrap and freeze them.

For full color photos and step by step visual instructions please visit www.daniellemporter.com/recipes

Photo Credits

ABOUT THE AUTHOR

A big mouth, Jesus loving, cupcake and kale eating, nutrition counselor, Danielle Porter, MPH shares her passion for helping other women come to see that their physical health journey is inseparable from their spiritual walk with Christ. As a world traveling Army wife and mother of 2, Danielle can often be found not trying to lose her ever-loving mind because she overcommitted herself in obedience to the Lord. She has helped hundreds of women reclaim their bodies in service to Christ.

https://www.teamnourished.com

https://www.daniellemPorter.com

Author photo used with permission of Kirsten Harr

Made in the USA
Monee, IL
12 March 2021